7

Breakthrough Biggies

How to Conquer Everyday Life Challenges and Create Transformation in Your Life!

KATHY MELA
Mindset Navigator

Mindset Navigator Books
HOLLYWOOD, FLORIDA

KATHY MELA
Mindset Navigator

Published by
Mindset Navigator Books
HOLLYWOOD, FLORIDA
www.KathyMela.com

ISBN: 978-0-69286-471-5

Cover and interior:
Gary A. Rosenberg • www.thebookcouple.com

Printed in the United States of America

Introduction

ONE LIFE!

That's what each of us has, one life to live to the fullest.

As I've traveled my own life journey, there have been twist and turns, hills and valleys, and bumps in the road. Each one of my experiences has brought me to this moment, writing this book.

This book was written to support you in creating transformation in your life.

It began when I started thinking about the most common challenges faced by people every day. Challenges like fear, overwhelm, and self-sabotage can paralyze us. It is imperative that we discover ways to move through these challenges in order to grow and flourish in our one AMAZING life.

I believe that the power to make changes in our lives lies in our head.

Thoughts become things.

What we think about we bring about.

Think about an area of your life where you've had success.

Prior to taking action to move you toward success, you "thought" about where you wanted to be and created action around what you thought.

This book is designed to give you some food for thought and then create awareness of where you are, where you want to go, and what action steps will get you there.

There is power in putting pen to paper as you connect with your own beliefs and perceptions, decide which beliefs are working for you and which perceptions you choose to change.

My intention for you in reading and working through this book is that you will be guided to possibility and awareness-thinking and create a life you'll love to live.

1
Fear

What is fear? I once heard someone refer to FEAR as False Evidence Appearing Real.

Or it can mean *Face Everything and Rise!* What are you afraid of? I'm afraid of heights, judgment, and not being able to care for myself physically and financially. What do you do about fear?

I believe we have to **feel the fear** and **PUSH** through it. I use visualization to see what's on the other side of the fear, to evaluate the cost and benefits of staying in fear or pushing through it. Being afraid of heights, I especially don't like escalators. I take every opportunity to get on an escalator and experience pushing through my fear. I challenge you today to pick one thing you're fearful of and take one action step to push through the fear.

*"He who fears something
gives it power over him."*
—MOORISH PROVERB

Extended Practice: BEING

B—Breakthrough to discover what you really want. Acknowledge one fear and decide what you want on the other side of that fear.

_____

_____

_____

_____

E—Examine why you want what you want. Why do you want to conquer this fear?

_____

_____

_____

_____

I—Investigate why you do not already have what you want. From a space of personal accountability, write why you haven't conquered this fear.

_____

_____

_____

_____

N—Next action: What strategy are you NOW going to use to get on the other side of this fear?

_____

_____

_____

_____

G—Get moving, what's your ONE next step. What is one action step you are willing to take TODAY to move you forward in your life around the fear you just acknowledged?

_____

_____

_____

_____

2
Resistance

Resistance is part of the 3 R's—resentment, resistance, revenge. As humans, we move through, in, and around these feelings quite often in life. I've spent a lot of time in resistance. I know I'm in resistance when I'm sarcastic, confused, angry, avoiding. It comes from not dealing with resentment.

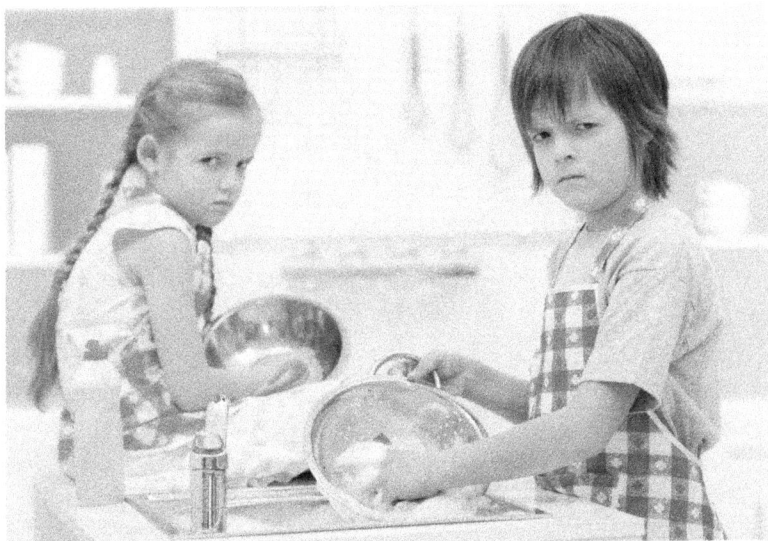

Resentment is any negative emotional reaction to *what you think* was said or done, whether or not it's true. Creating awareness is key to move through it. Now, when I notice my resistance to something, I face it, use open honest communication, forgiveness and release it and move on. I challenge you today to take one action step that allows you to take notice of where you have resistance in your life.

*"People don't resist change.
They resist being changed."*
—PETER M. SENGE

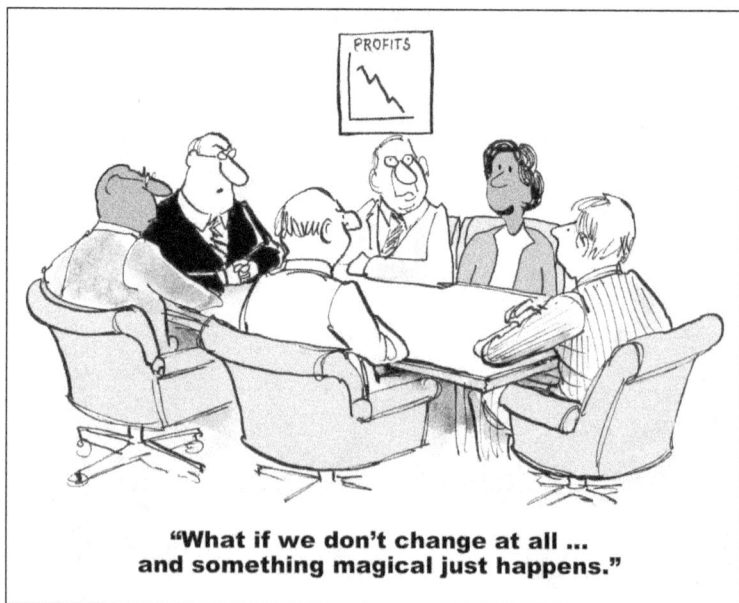

**"What if we don't change at all ...
and something magical just happens."**

Extended Practice: BEING

B—Breakthrough to discover what you really want. Acknowledge one area in your life where you notice resistance and decide what you want on the other side of that resistance.

_____

_____

_____

_____

E—Examine why you want what you want. Why do you want to conquer this resistance?

_____

_____

_____

_____

I—Investigate why you do not already have what you want. From a space of personal accountability, write why you haven't conquered this area of resistance in your life.

_____

_____

_____

_____

N—Next action: What strategy are you NOW going to use to get on the other side of this resistance?

_____

_____

_____

_____

G—Get moving, what's your ONE next step. What is one action step you are willing to take TODAY to move you forward in your life around the area of resistance you just acknowledged?

_____

_____

_____

_____

If you limit your choices only to what seems possible or reasonable, you disconnect yourself from what you truly want. And all that is left is compromise.

3

Compromise

Sometimes in life I say or do things that are more in alignment with other people's wishes or perspectives. This is a compromise of me, my values, my beliefs, who I am. Here's an example: I want to hang a picture. I decide which picture I like and where I want to hang it so I can see it often. Then I start thinking—well, I wonder what my friend will think.

Will she like it? Maybe she'll think it should go somewhere else. When really I know where I want it and I'm the one who will see it most. It's important to know what I want and what's in alignment with me in every area of my life. The question is: If I'm doing this with something as simple as where to hang a picture, where else am I doing this in my life, in my job, in my business, in my relationships? Where are *YOU* doing this in your life? I challenge you today to discover one area where you consistently make compromises and take one action step to BE in alignment with who you are.

> *"Compromise is a stalling*
> *between two fools."*
> —STEPHEN FRY

Extended Practice: BEING

B—Breakthrough to discover what you really want. Think of one area in your life where you compromise yourself and your values. What do you want instead of the compromise?

_____

_____

_____

_____

E—Examine why you want what you want. Why do you want to conquer compromising yourself and your values?

_____

_____

_____

_____

I—Investigate why you do not already have what you want. From a space of personal accountability, write why you allow this form of compromise in your life.

_____

_____

_____

_____

N—Next action: What strategy are you NOW going to use to get on the other side of this area of compromise?

_____

_____

_____

_____

G—Get moving, what's your ONE next step. What is one action step you are willing to take TODAY to move you forward in this specific area of compromise?

_____

_____

_____

_____

"Say no to everything, so you can say yes to the ONE thing."
—RICHIE NORTON

4
Saying Yes When Meaning No

Have you ever said yes to something when you really wanted to say no? Why?

Why do we say yes when we mean no? We do it for many reasons. What's really important to remember is that when we say yes and mean no, we give away our power. It's important to know our value and worth and stand in our own power. This can be done with love and compassion. I challenge you today to **mean yes when you say yes** and **say no when you mean no.**

"It takes effort to say no when our heart and brains and guts and, most important, pride are yearning to say yes. Practice."

—COLE HARMONSON, *PRE MIDDLE AGE: 40 LESSONS IN GROWING THE HELL UP*

"Let today mark a new beginning for you.
Give yourself permission to say NO
without feeling guilty, mean, or selfish.
Anybody who gets upset and/or
expects you to say YES all of the
time clearly doesn't have your
best interest at heart.
Always remember: You have a right to say
NO without having to explain yourself.
Be at peace with your decisions."

—STEPHANIE LAHART

Extended Practice: BEING

B—Breakthrough to discover what you really want. Acknowledge one area of your life where you often say yes when you mean no.

_____

_____

_____

_____

E—Examine why you want what you want. Why do you want to conquer this habit of saying yes when you mean no?

_____

_____

_____

_____

I—Investigate why you do not already have what you want. From a space of personal accountability, write why you say yes when you mean no.

_____

_____

_____

_____

N—Next action: What strategy are you NOW going to use to say yes when you mean yes and no when you mean no?

_____

_____

_____

_____

G—Get moving, what's your ONE next step. What is one action step you are willing to take TODAY to say what you mean?

_____

_____

_____

_____

5
Overcommitting

Do you overcommit? I think we all do at times. What does it mean to overcommit? For me I've become aware of a tendency to take on many projects at one time. I'm often left feeling overworked, underappreciated, and stressed to the max!

I once thought this tendency was a character trait I possessed. I discovered it's not! It's a belief system, and belief systems can be changed. I'm the one who has control over what I think, say, and do. What about you? What's really the underlying thread that allows anyone to overcommit on a regular basis? I challenge you today to take one action step that will create awareness around why you overcommit.

> *"Your beliefs become your thoughts,*
> *Your thoughts become your words,*
> *Your words become your actions,*
> *Your actions become your habits,*
> *Your habits become your values,*
> *Your values become your destiny."*
> —MAHATMA GANDHI

Extended Practice: BEING

B—Breakthrough to discover what you really want. Acknowledge one area of your life where you over-commit.

_____

_____

_____

_____

E—Examine why you want what you want. Why do you want to conquer overcommitting?

_____

_____

_____

_____

I—Investigate why you do not already have what you want. From a space of personal accountability, write why you continue to overcommit.

_____

_____

_____

_____

N—Next Action: What strategy are you NOW going to use to break the overcommit habit?

_____

_____

_____

_____

G—Get moving, what's your ONE next step. What is one action step you are willing to take TODAY to move you forward in the area of overcommitting?

_____

_____

_____

_____

6
Self-Sabotage

What does self-sabotage mean? Self-sabotage is a behavior pattern that is in conflict with your personality. These behaviors can be serious. However, the context I am referring to today are those behaviors that are subtle self-sabotaging behaviors.

One of my patterns centers around my sleep habits. I often push myself to stay up in order to "get it all done," which creates a circle of decreased productivity and low energy. I actually care for myself and alter my behavior pattern when I honor my body's need for rest and relaxation. I challenge you today to identify one of your self-sabotaging behaviors and decide on one action step to alter your behavior.

"Self-sabotage is when we say we want something and then go about making sure it doesn't happen."
—ALYCE P. CORNYN-SELBY

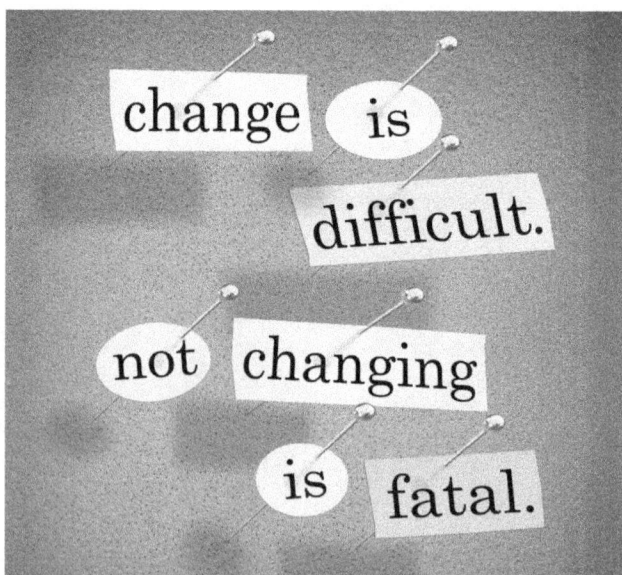

change is difficult. not changing is fatal.

Extended Practice: BEING

B—Breakthrough to discover what you really want. Acknowledge one area in your life where you self-sabotage.

_____

_____

_____

_____

E—Examine why you want what you want. Why do you want to conquer self-sabotage?

_____

_____

_____

_____

I—Investigate why you do not already have what you want. From a space of personal accountability, write why you haven't conquered self-sabotage.

_____

_____

_____

_____

N—Next Action: What strategy are you NOW going to use to stop self-sabotaging?

_____

_____

_____

_____

G—Get moving, what's your ONE next step. What is one action step you are willing to take TODAY to move you forward in your life around self-sabotaging?

_____

_____

_____

_____

7

Being Stuck

What does it mean to BE STUCK? Have you ever had a song stuck in your head? You keep hearing or singing the same lyrics over and over. That's what it's like to have something stuck in your mind. What does it mean to be stuck in your life? Are you in a job you no longer love? Are you stuck in a living arrangement you no longer want to be in? Are you stuck in a mindset or belief system? Being stuck means standing still, not moving, not growing.

What do you do when you're stuck? What's worked for me is to reach out, connect, and seek support. Get a little help from my coach, mentor, friends. I challenge you today to take one action step to move out of an area where you feel stuck.

"The only thing that feels worse than being stuck in a situation that makes you unhappy is realizing that you are not ready or willing *to change whatever it is."*
—ASHLY LORENZANA

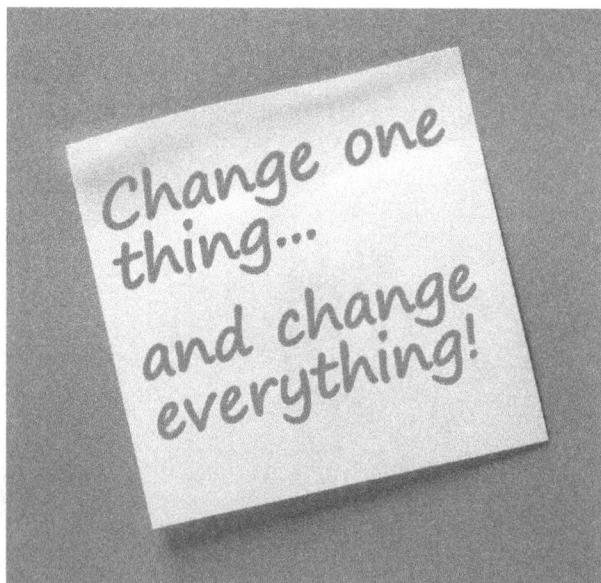

Extended Practice: BEING

B—Breakthrough to discover what you really want. Acknowledge one area of your life where you feel stuck.

_____

_____

_____

_____

E—Examine why you want what you want. Why do you want to get unstuck?

_____

_____

_____

_____

I—Investigate why you do not already have what you want. From a space of personal accountability, write why you are still stuck in this area.

_____

_____

_____

_____

N—Next Action: What strategy are you NOW going to use to get unstuck in this one area?

_____

_____

_____

_____

G—Get moving, what's your ONE next step. What is one action step you are willing to take TODAY to BE FREE in this area?

_____

_____

_____

_____

Closing Thoughts

It is my sincere passion and vision to see *every* human being **grow and flourish** in their one amazing life!

My objective in creating this book is to present you with concepts that may support you in transforming areas of your life that are no longer working for you.

Our beliefs and perceptions define our sense of the world around us and they may not always represent the actual truth.

This belief system is your *story*—your perception of your life experience. You are in charge of your story and you get the opportunity to rewrite it whenever you choose to create a life you'll love to live!

About Kathy

Kathy Mela is an author, speaker, thought transformer, business leader, mindset coach, and entrepreneur. Her promise is to guide you in possibility and awareness thinking. She offers support in discovering your answers and creating your roadmap for your life.

Kathy practices being mindfully present and will fully listen and encourage YOU to move more powerfully through this journey called LIFE!

Contact her at www.kathymela.com

www.ingramcontent.com/pod-product-compliance
Lightning Source LLC
Chambersburg PA
CBHW031336040426
42443CB00005B/369